THE NORTH AND SOUTH POLE?:
K12 LIFE SCIENCE SERIES

SPEEDY
PUBLISHING

Speedy Publishing LLC
40 E. Main St. #1156
Newark, DE 19711
www.speedypublishing.com

Copyright 2015

The two poles are at extreme opposites of the planet, and many of their features are also polar opposites.

NORTH POLE

The North Pole is the northernmost point on the Earth, lying diametrically opposite the South Pole.

A number of different types of animals make their home in the arctic, including polar bears, birds, walrus and seals.

There is no land at the North Pole, it is covered in a thick layer of ice around 6 to 9 feet thick.

SOUTH POLE

The South Pole is the southernmost point on the Earth. From the South Pole, all directions are north.

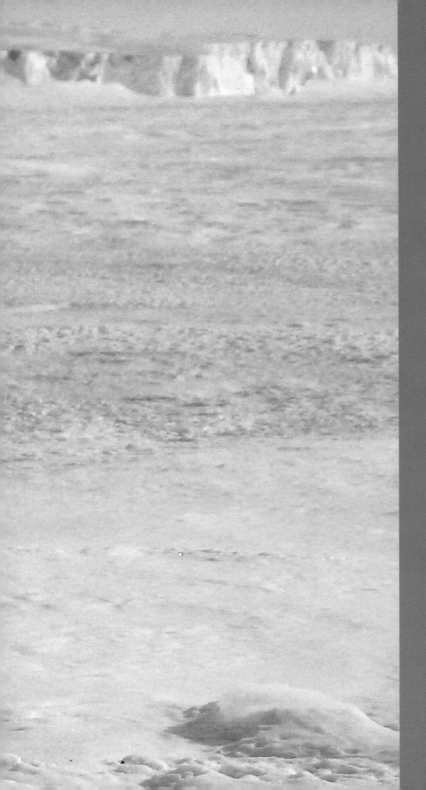

The South Pole is located on Antarctica, one of the Earth's seven continents. Antarctica is the coldest, windiest, and driest place on earth.

Most of the animals of Antarctica live on the edge and coast or in the water surrounding the continent.

48713664R00020